EDINBURGH
PAST & PRESENT

A pictorial record of the ancient City of Edinburgh

C. S. MINTO and N. E. S. ARMSTRONG

©1975 Oxford Illustrated Press, Norma Armstrong and C. S. Minto

Printed in Hong Kong by South China Printing Company

First edition, hardback 1975
                paperback 1979
Reprinted 1980

ISBN 0 902280 71 6

OXFORD ILLUSTRATED PRESS
Shelley Close Risinghurst Oxford

ntroduction

Edinburgh has always been a city of contrasts, scenery, chitecture, culture and history all presenting infinite riety. Her physical setting ranges from the hilly landscape the Pentland, Braid and Blackford Hills to the coastal enery of the Firth of Forth. Balancing the haphazard closes d wynds of the Old Town, the New Town stands in its nned Georgian elegance. The city which produced Sir alter Scott and Robert Louis Stevenson produced William Gonagall too. As capital of Scotland, Edinburgh has been scene of many important national events including John ox thundering reformation from his pulpit in St. Giles, ry Queen of Scots, the ill-starred Stuart queen, entering city in triumph in 1561, James VI her son leaving his ace at Holyroodhouse with his court in 1603 to become g of the United Kingdom and Prince Charles Edward art with his highlanders capturing the city in 1745. cholars disagree about the origin of the city's name but sixth-century Welsh poem, the *Goddodin* offers a likely anation, describing the area where the Castle now stands Dineidin', 'the fort at Edin'. Dineidin later became n-Eideann' in Gaelic and finally Edinburgh. We do have ence that there has been a fort of some description from arliest times on the volcanic Castle rock. Providing ral protection, the Castle is the reason for the burgh's ence and early settlements grew up in its shadow. ntemporary charters indicate that there was the nings of a town from the late eleventh or early twelfth ry and one can picture the early burgesses developing little strips of land, with houses facing the main street gardens behind. Gradually the houses spread down the leading towards another volcanic rock known as r's Seat. As the population grew more houses were built he gardens disappeared, resulting in the pattern of tecture so typical of Old Edinburgh. Maps of the nth century show a compact burgh protected on three by the city wall with its five gates, or ports as they are in Scotland. To the west stood the Castle over- wing the High Street and Cowgate, with many closes ynds running at right angles. To the north, completing rgh's defences, lies the man-made Nor' Loch which its part in so many escapes from the Castle. To the he Netherbow Port leads to the burgh of Canongate e Palace of Holyroodhouse and the Abbey within its cts.

historical and economic reasons, Edinburgh remained ed within her walls for almost two hundred years. expansion was necessary it was upwards rather than ds and soaring 'lands' or tenements of sixteen storeys mmonplace. One can visualise this bustling, dirty, wded town of 48,000 people with aristocrats, judges, nts and working classes living cheek by jowl in their nth-century skyscrapers. There had been no real effort d the burgh, although there had been some tary exercises in town planning with the building of Square about 1746, Alison Square in 1750 and Brown in 1763. A solitary plan to build outside the wall to

the south had resulted in the building of George Square in 1766.

It was little wonder that the Scottish burghs could not consider expansion programmes. The Act of Union in 1707, removing the Parliament to London had repercussions throughout the country. In addition the turbulent upheaval of the Jacobite Rebellions of 1715 and 1745 hardly made for national stability. Edinburgh was no longer a capital city and many of the influential families moved south.

Yet at this very time when the city seemed to be at its lowest ebb, the thread of apparent irrationality which runs right through her history became visible again. In the 1750s several men of vision led by Lord Provost George Drummond began to discuss the possibility of expanding the city to the north. Incredible as it seems these enlightened men planned to build a new town of a size and beauty quite unknown in Scotland, a town with no shops or businesses. Perhaps the most remarkable feature was that each family was to have a house of its own, not sharing flats with a common entrance as had been the practice in the Old Town. In preparation for this considerable architectural and engineering feat, the Nor' Loch had been partially drained in 1763 and the necessity for access between the two towns had been anticipated with the planning of the North Bridge. In 1767 the Town Council advertised an architectural competition for a new town in the fields to the north of the Old Town. This was won by James Craig, a young Scots architect, and his design resulted in a grid-iron plan with a square at each end (St. Andrew Square to the east and Charlotte Square to the west), the main streets being Princes Street, George Street and Queen Street. It is interesting to speculate on the designs submitted by other competitors, for although the feuing plan and Craig's plan still survive, there is no trace of the others.

Building began on the first 'New Town' in 1767 and over the years successive plans were developed to the north, east and west of Craig's plan and by about 1831 the area we know as Georgian Edinburgh was completed. Coinciding with this exciting architectural venture was an equally exciting intellectual resurgence. With Adam Smith, David Hume, Robert Fergusson, Robert Burns, Sir Walter Scott, Alexander Runciman, Alexander Nasmyth and Sir Henry Raeburn living and working in the city, Edinburgh was indeed enjoying a Golden Age.

The exodus of the aristocracy, the professional and merchant classes to the New Town, left behind a working-class ghetto in the Old Town. The flats were sub-divided and official reports of the mid-nineteenth century tell us of High Street tenements in which 248 people were living in 59 rooms with no running water or sanitation; so co-existent with the splendours of the New Town, Edinburgh had some of the worst slums in Europe. A turning point came in 1862 with the appointment of the first medical officer of health, which was directly due to the 'Heave Awa' Land' disaster when a High Street tenement building collapsed killing 35 of the occupants. Eventually social reform in housing, education, medicine and working conditions, touched the lives of the Old Town inhabitants, with the result that many of them moved away from this environment to yet another Edinburgh which was spreading beyond the New Town towards the shores of the Forth and south towards the Pentlands. Some of them, for example, built their own homes in co-operative building schemes; others rented working-men's houses built for them along the line of the railway and in the industrial areas; others again moved to the south to the vast new tenement areas growing up on the ancient Burgh Muir.

Walking about the streets of Edinburgh today, this history can still be traced. The Castlehill, Lawnmarket and High Street of the Old Town is the upper half of the modern Royal Mile and the ancient burgh of Canongate forms its lower half. The name 'Royal Mile', although twentieth century in origin is an apt description of this street, which has been so closely connected with the nobility and royalty of Scotland. The 'Mile' is accurate too because the distance from the drawbridge of the Castle to the entrance door of the Palace of Holyroodhouse is just over a mile. Much of Edinburgh's story is embodied in this street particularly in the Castle, from which the city grew, and Holyroodhouse (the palace of the ancient Scottish kings started in the sixteenth century) is still a royal residence. Thanks to the rebuilding and restoration programmes of the Town Council, this street, which was a slum in the nineteenth century, has returned in the twentieth century to a lively area, with shops and houses for people of a wide range of interests and professions, much as it was in the eighteenth century. Craig's New Town can still be recognised in modern Edinburgh, although the original intention to exclude shops and businesses has been completely reversed. Princes Street has become one of the best-known shopping streets in the world, St. Andrew Square a centre for banking and insurance and Charlotte Square, although the finest remaining example of Georgian architecture in the city, has many offices. With the recent formation of a New Town Conservation Committee, Edinburgh is ensuring that an important part of Europe's architectural heritage will be preserved.

Edinburgh now has a population of approximately 450,000 and the modern city is an interesting mixture of Old Town, New Town, nineteenth-century tenements and villas, twentieth-century bungalows and slums; together with several villages which have managed to retain part of their original identity. The city's traditional industries of printing, publishing and papermaking are still flourishing, and reflected in the many old and new schools, colleges and universities is the traditional Scots desire for education. Since 1947 Edinburgh has been host every year to an International Festival of Music and Drama, yet again providing a contrast between the formality of the official festival and the youthful informality of the fringe. In common with most present day cities, Edinburgh has problems including overcrowding, unemployment, vandalism and traffic congestion. In the past few years there have been several controversial issues, for example the siting of a second runway for Turnhouse Airport, the proposed building of an inner-ring road and the design of an opera house. The conflict of opinions activated by these issues is absolutely typical of the ever-present spirit of contrast. We hope we have managed to convey in our choice of photographs, some part of this atmosphere which permeates the city and gives it its beauty and vitality.

N.E.S. ARMSTRONG

List of Illustrations

ACKNOWLEDGEMENTS

The inestimable help of my co-author in making the ch
the original photographs from the extensive files maint
by the Edinburgh City Libraries is most gratefully
acknowledged. The authors recognise that without the
willingly offered help of the City Librarian, Mr. J. Alan
this book would not have been possible and wish to exp
him their primary thanks for allowing the use of the Ce
Library's local history resources. A great debt too, is ov
the hotels at either end of Princes Street, the North Bri
the Rutland, for allowing photographs to be taken from
premises. H.M. Register House also offered willing ass
towards obtaining an equivalent photograph of the blo
buildings at the 'East End'. This photograph of the ear
is of considerable technical interest, having been taken
short a focus lens on a 10" x 10" field camera that the
wide angle lens fell far short of a similar performance.

C.S. MINTO

1. GRASSMARKET, South Side

The south side of the Grassmarket was totally different in character from the north side, mainly because most of it had been pulled down and re-built at intervals before 1879 leaving little of the vernacular architecture. The building with the clock tower was the 'new' Corn Exchange designed by David Cousin and built in 1849. It was the third site which the Corn Exchange had occupied in the Grassmarket.

In 1968 the Corn Exchange and the British Linen Bank were replaced by the Mountbatten Building housing the Faculty of Humanities and the Faculty of Electrical and Electronic Engineering of Heriot-Watt University. The seven storey building has a tower block, whose height was restricted to protect the view from the Castle Esplanade. Founded by Leonard Horner in 1821 the School of Arts expanded till it became Heriot-Watt University in 1966. At the moment the various faculties are housed in scattered buildings but they will eventually all be sited at the new campus under construction at Riccarton.

2. GRASSMARKET, East

At the east end, the Grassmarket joins the West Bow, the main western approach to the Old Town. The gallows stood near the lampost on the right. Here many Covenanters, dying for their religion, met their death, and many criminals were publicly executed. The most incredible execution must have been that of 'Half-Hangit Maggie Dickson' in 1724, who after being 'hanged' was cut down by her friends and put in her coffin. The body was conveyed by cart to her home, a few miles east of the city. The jolting of the cart revived her, and by the time the mourners reached Musselburgh the 'Corpse' was sitting up in her coffin. The gallows have gone by 1904, but the Bow Well, built in 1681, still stands.

Many of the tenements in the West Bow have been rebuilt and are now attractive flats, but there are still reminders of the sad social outcasts, who form part of the Grassmarket population, in the Greyfriars Hotel and the Grassmarket Mission.

3. CANDLEMAKER ROW

Joining Bristo to the Cowgate and the Grassmarket, Candlemaker Row takes its name from the Incorporation of Candlemakers, whose hall stands in this area. The Row overlooks Greyfriars Churchyard which has an interesting collection of tombstones, some of which can be seen sticking up over the wall on the south side of the street. Here in 1890 some of the early domestic buildings are still standing, although the Cunzie House, the Old Scottish Mint, which stood here in the 16th century during the regency of Mary of Guise, has disappeared. Some efforts were being made at street cleaning as can be seen by the presence of a dustman with his horse and cart.

Taken on a clearer day the modern view gives a glimpse of the Castle. A new wall reveals more of Greyfriars Churchyard especially as the old houses have been removed. This is a district of down-and-outs with a number of lodging houses like the Greyfriars Hotel at the Cowgatehead.

4. HOPE HOUSE, Cowgate

Standing close to the central pier of George IV Bridge, the Hope House was the home of Sir Thomas Hope, King's Advocate of Charles I in 1626. The mansion was one of the finest of its day, with a grand oak staircase and two carved lintels with the mottoes 'Tecum Habita, 1616' (keep at home) and 'At Hospes Humo' (an anagram of Sir Thomas's name). By 1880 the mansion has lost its ancient grandeur and was Ramsay's lodging house. Above the ornamental rail of the bridge the Sheriff Court House can be seen on the east side of George IV Bridge. Taken from the Cowgatehead the modern view shows, in place of the Hope House, the Central Library opened in 1890. Sir Thomas has not been forgotten because his two lintels have been built into doorways in the library. On the opposite side of the Cowgate we get a glimpse of the steeple of the Magdalene Chapel, the 16th century chapel of the Incorporation of Hammermen, which contains the only pre-Reformation glass in Edinburgh.

5. BANK STREET

Taken in the 1930s from the Lawnmarket, the older view shows Bank Street and the Bank of Scotland. The Bank was completed in 1806 after considerable difficulties, as it stands on the steep slope leading down to the valley of the Nor' Loch. Bank Street is the continuation of the Mound, joining the Old Town to the New Town. The buildings on the right are being demolished to make way for the Sheriff Court. For a time the Court had been held in the Old County Buildings opposite, and had moved to new premises designed by David Bryce in 1868 in nearby George IV Bridge. The passing of the road traffic Act had increased litigation to such a degree that by the 1930s Bryce's building was quite inadequate.

The island site bounded by the Lawnmarket, St Giles Street, and Bank Street was, therefore, acquired, and the new Sheriff Court opened in 1937. On the opposite corner there is a reminder of the inimitable Deacon Brodie, the 18th century locksmith and burglar, in Deacon Brodie's Tavern.

6. THE ROYAL EXCHANGE

Completed in 1761 the Royal Exchange was the first public building in the 18th century improvement schemes. Finding that the city merchants still preferred to transact their business in the streets, the Town Council took over part of the building in 1811 as a Council Chamber. Gradually the building became the hub of local government and was renamed the City Chambers. The appearance of the fine piazza *c* 1880 is completely spoiled by the shops crammed into the entrance archways. The adjacent buildings illustrate very well the towering tenements of the High Street with their forestairs. The extensions to the City Chambers swept away three of the old tenement blocks but the remaining facade, towards Cockburn Street, is little changed. It is not evident from the photographs, but from the front entrance of the City Chambers to its back door in Cockburn Street, there is a drop of sixty-five feet. Consequently some of the closes have been preserved intact beneath the building.

7. NORTH BRIDGE

Several of the shops on the North Bridge are being closed down *c* 1898 and the Bon Marché on the corner of the High Street is having a great removal sale. From this angle we can see Allan Ramsay's House in the High Street, described in detail in No 8. Clearly a demolition scheme is under way. The shops and Allan Ramsay's house are being cleared to make way for Patrick Thomson's Department Store which was opened in 1906. The department store now occupies most of the block, apart from the corner section, which is the Royal Bank of Scotland, and the part at the far end occupied by the Carlton Hotel. At this point the North Bridge meets the South Bridge and the two form a popular shopping area, known locally as 'the Bridges'.

8. ALLAN RAMSAY'S HOUSE

This picturesque group of buildings stood on the north side of the High Street near its junction with the North Bridge. The building with the forestair was the house and shop of Allan Ramsay, the wig-maker who became a poet and bookseller. From this shop in 1721 he was publishing books with the imprint 'At the sign of the Mercury'. His business was so successful that by 1728 he had moved to better premises in the Luckenbooths, near St Giles, further up the High Street. The well was one of the four main public wells in the Old Town, removed in the 1960s.

The whole block was demolished *c* 1898 and the site is now occupied by the Royal Bank of Scotland, and Patrick Thomson's Store. It is ironical that this area, once given over to temperance hotels, now has three pubs and a bookmaker close by.

9. JOHN KNOX'S HOUSE

John Knox's House, on the north side of the High Street, is known to every tourist to the city. Strictly speaking the house belonged to James Mossman, goldsmith to Mary Queen of Scots. When Knox returned to Edinburgh in August 1572, he was a dying man. His manse in Warriston Close was not considered suitable for an invalid, and so he moved into Mossman's house. Knox died in November of that year, so in reality his connection with the house was very short. Nevertheless there is a small museum there reached by the forestair.

To the west of the house stands Moubray House, another early building with a forestair, and beside it the Fountain Well. To the east stands the Moray-Knox Church, and in the distance the tenements of the Canongate, including Morocco Land, are visible.

Both Moubray House and John Knox's House have been completely restored. Moray-Knox Church has been pulled down, and in its place in 1972 the Church of Scotland opened a small theatre called the 'Netherbow'.

10. CHESSELL'S COURT

This print shows Chessell's Court, one of the open courtyards on the south side of the Canongate as it looked in the 18th century. The Excise Office stood here and during a raid on this building, justice finally caught up with one of the city's most enterprising characters. Deacon Brodie was deacon of the locksmiths and a respectable businessman by day. By night, trading on his highly specialised knowledge of locks and keys, he was the leader of a very successful gang of burglars. The gang were surprised in the Excise Office and all of them captured except the Deacon who managed to escape abroad. He was eventually captured and executed on a new gibbet which ironically he had designed himself. All traces of the Excise Office and Deacon Brodie have gone from the Canongate, although Robert Louis Stevenson has immortalised Brodie by basing 'Dr Jekyll and Mr Hyde' on his life.

Chessell's Court is perhaps the most successful of the Town Council's restoration schemes.

11. CANONGATE TOLBOOTH

Just opposite Huntly House stands the 16th century Canongate Tolbooth — at one time the council house and prison of the ancient burgh of Canongate. The burgh was named after the Canons of Holyrood who took this 'gait', or way, when walking from the Castle to their Abbey at Holyrood. Most of the buildings adjoining the Tolbooth were put up during the 19th century improvement schemes. Most of them sport the Old Town 'flags' — washing hanging from the windows on poles.

The Tolbooth, now a city museum, has altered very little. It is used mainly for exhibitions. A recent exhibit can be seen at the pavement's edge; the bailie's lamp was part of an Edinburgh Festival exhibition 'Aince a Bailie'. A bailie is a senior member of the Town Council, who, in Edinburgh, is specially honoured by having an ornamental lamp put up outside his home. The buildings west of the Tolbooth show how Edinburgh Corporation has improved the old tenements. Known as Bible Land and Shoemakers' Land, they were rebuilt in 1957.

12. HUNTLY HOUSE

Standing in Bakehouse Close in the
Canongate, Huntly House takes its name
from its connection with the Marquess of
Huntly in the 16th century, but by 1907 it
had deteriorated from a town house into a
slum. Shops were built into the lower floor,
one of which 'Poets' Box' sold the popular
songs of the period. For just one penny you
could learn the words of 'Never Push a Man
Because He's Going Down the Hill' or
'Paddy McGinty's Goat'.

The Town Council acquired the property
in 1924 taking infinite pains with its
restoration as can be seen in the modern
photograph. It was opened in 1932 as
Huntly House Museum, which has
developed over the years into an excellent
museum of local history where, without
paying anything at all you can learn a great
deal about the history, life and crafts of
Edinburgh.

13. WHITEHORSE CLOSE

Surely one of the most attractive of the Royal Mile Closes, Whitehorse Close stands on the north side of the Canongate, not far from Holyroodhouse. The central building was Whitehorse Inn, a well-known coaching establishment, in which, according to Sir Walter Scott in *Waverley*, Prince Charlie's officers were quartered when they captured the city in 1745. The coaches for London, which took 'eight days God willing' to reach the capital, left from the stables at the rear of the inn. In 1870 the Close was dilapidated but became even more derelict before it was restored by Edinburgh Corporation in 1965.

It is interesting to see how the architects have restored the houses, removing the forestairs at each side, but retaining the character of the original group of buildings.

14. ABBEY STRAND

The Abbey Strand is at the foot of the Canongate immediately outside Holyroodhouse, which can be seen in the distance beside the ruins of Holyrood Abbey. In 1914 it was still a residential area with a public house, and shops. The whitewash on the entrance to the close and on the sides of the buildings is a reminder of the efforts of Sir Henry Littlejohn, Edinburgh's first medical officer of health, when he started to bring about improvements in the Old Town. Now beautifully rebuilt, the old tenement has been lowered and extra dormer windows added.

The clutter of little shops has been removed and a garden laid out, including Queen Mary's Bath House, making an attractive approach to the Palace. Outside the tenement three S's set in the roadway commemorate the entrance to the Abbey Sanctuary where debtors taking refuge from their pursuers were given the sarcastic name 'Abbey Lairds'.

15. WEST END

What ever became of 'Epps's Cocoa'? Many
of the cable cars including this one at the
'West End' carried a large advertisement,
but the name is quite unfamiliar today. The
'West End' is the West End of Princes
Street, where Lothian Road, Hope Street,
Queensferry Street and Shandwick Place
converge. Looking towards Princes Street we
can see St John's Episcopal Church and the
spire of St Cuthbert's, with the Castle in the
mist behind. On the left-hand corner stood
Maule's, a large department store, and on
the right-hand corner, at Lothian Road, the
Caledonian Station. The station is still there
today although disused since 1965.

The Castle, St Cuthbert's and St John's
are all quite unmoved by the passage of
time, but Maule's has given place to Binn's,
another department store. Its controversial
clock decorated with highlanders, is much
beloved by tourists, but less popular with the
natives. The old clock has gone too, but is
still in use in the centre of a roundabout at
London Road.

16. PRINCES STREET, looking east

Looking east from the Rutland Hotel this view of 1946 gives an excellent impression of the proportions of Princes Street, with the vast range of shops on one side, and the gardens on the other.

Comparing it with the view of 1974 we find that although the architecture of the block between the West End and South Charlotte Street is practically unchanged, the shops and their tenants are. The Bank of Scotland now occupies the British Linen Bank premises, the American Express takes the place of Duncan Flockhart, the chemist, Wilson and Sharp, the jewellers, are still in the same shop, and the adjoining bookshop, once occupied by McNiven and Wallace, was, until recently, Menzies West End Bookshop. The biggest change is on the corner where the well-known baker, MacVitties Guest, has been replaced by British European Airways.

There is surprisingly little alteration to the West End, as a whole, the major changes having taken place in the centre and East End of Princes Street.

17. CENTRAL PRINCES STREET

How incredible it seems — all that parking space on Princes Street, but it's 1920 and private cars are still a luxury. The chauffeur standing by the open tourer is waiting for his master, who may be shopping at Hamilton and Inches, the jewellers, or visiting the New Club. A cable tram goes rattling along towards Pilrig, and taxis seem readily available. All the familiar landmarks can be seen in this view from the west, the Royal Scottish Academy, the pinnacle of the Scott Monument, the North British Hotel clock, the Nelson Column and the National Monument.

Princes Street is now a 'no waiting' area and the tram lines covered by a central island where the pedestrians can take refuge from the traffic when crossing. The new shopping blocks replacing the New Club and the Life Assurance building have an upper street level as it is intended to have two-level shopping when Princes Street is completely rebuilt. Queen Victoria and the sphinxes still sit serenely on top of the Royal Scottish Academy.

18. PRINCES STREET, 1946

Taken in 1946 this view of Princes Street from the foot of the Mound, conveys the feeling of post-war austerity in the uniformity of the cars and the severity of the women's clothes. Tram cars were the principal form of public transport and remained in use till 1956. It shows part of the facade of the Life Association building, the New Club and a few blocks along the Balmoral Restaurant, a favourite tea-room run by the well-known firm R and T Gibson. Particularly noticeable are the patterns of the granite setts which covered all Edinburgh's roads.

In 1974 the aspect is more cheerful with the light new buildings. The girls in the foreground are probably touring Scotland and making for the Waverley Station. A fleet of double decker buses negotiates Princes Street in an obstacle race of traffic lights and jay-walking pedestrians. The Life Association, The New Club and the Balmoral Restaurant have all gone, the first two replaced by several little shops and the last by Littlewood's Stores.

PRINCES STREET, WEST OF HANOVER STREET, *circa* 1860.

19. PRINCES STREET at Hanover Street

Visiting Edinburgh in 1860 one would immediately notice the contrasting styles of architecture in Princes Street. On the corner of Hanover Street one of the original Georgian buildings was standing, incorporating the shops of James Stillie, the bookseller, and Thornton and Co. A few doors along stood the splendid Life Association Building, designed by David Rhind and newly completed in 1858, and next to it the New Club. If tired, the visitor could take a seat or a stroll in Princes Street Gardens, or perhaps visit the Royal Scottish Academy, whose ornamental lamps can be seen on the left.

The corner of Hanover Street has certainly changed, Collingwood, the jeweller, and the Australian Centre occupy most of the building, but the shape of the Old Georgian house is still recognisable, as is the adjoining block. But what has become of the Life Association and the New Club? After bitter controversy both were demolished and replaced by a complex of shops, including Halford's and Mothercare.

20. PRINCES STREET, East of the Mound

It's ten past three on a hot afternoon in 1903. The ladies with straw boaters and parasols take the air in Princes Street, strolling past the solid Victorian facades of the North British & Mercantile Insurance Company and the Royal Hotel to have afternoon tea in Jenners. A four-in-hand makes its leisurely journey to the Forth Bridge and a cable tram with its unprotected cargo is bound for Gorgie.

On a cold afternoon in 1974, Princes Street has changed considerably. Women in trouser-suits hurry briskly along. Many of the family shops have disappeared, swallowed up by the great multiples like British Home Stores and Marks and Spencer, but the upper floors of the two central blocks and Jenners remain very much as before. Everywhere the press of city traffic is reflected in road signs and restrictions. Double-decker buses carry their loads to Corstorphine, Morningside, Slateford, Cramond — indeed every part of the city.

21. SCOTT MONUMENT, looking north

This fine print by Joseph Ebsworth shows the view from the Scott Monument in 1846 looking north up South St David Street towards St Andrew Square and the Melville Column. It is packed with absorbing detail showing the original facades of the Princes Street buildings with 'areas' reached by steps. Particularly interesting on the west side is the shop front of Kennington and Jenner. On the roof of the first block on the east side is a photographer taking a family group. He is almost certainly James Howie who had his studio at 45 Princes Street.

The past hundred years have changed the face of this street called, as a joke, 'St David Street', after one of its early occupants, David Hume. Kennington and Jenner has become the well-known department store, Jenners occupying the whole block on the west side with two insurance company blocks behind, the Scottish Provident and the Scottish Widows. The view over St Andrew Square is blocked by the height of the Old Waverley Hotel but the top of the Melville Column can be seen over the roofs.

22. SCOTT MONUMENT, looking south

If one had the energy to climb the Scott Monument in 1875 this is the view that would meet the eye, looking south towards the Old Town: the lines of the North British Railway converging on the Waverley Station and the Waverley Bridge forming another link, via Cockburn Street, between the Old and New Towns. The background looks too theatrical to be real, with the line of Market Street, called after the fruit and vegetable market, and behind that the ridge of the High Street, with the crown steeple of St Giles and the spire of the Tron Kirk.

Reconstructed in 1895 the Waverley Station has been roofed over and the bridge slightly altered. This modern view also gives a glimpse, over the rooftops, of Arthur's Seat, Edinburgh's volcano (happily extinct) and of one of the spans of the North Bridge.

23. SCOTT MONUMENT, looking east

The Scott Monument was a favourite vantage point for the 19th century photographers.

The collection of monuments on the Calton Hill partially explains why Edinburgh was called 'The Athens of the North'. Just behind Dunlop the Hatters, the Martyrs' Monument in the Old Calton Cemetery is visible. On the Calton Hill itself, the Nelson Column stands by the National Monument, built in memory of those killed in the Napoleonic Wars. The next group includes the Playfair Monument, the temple-like memorial to Dugald Stewart, the City Observatory and in front of it Observatory House.

After being used for many years for exhibitions, flower shows and carnivals, the Waverley Market is being demolished and a conference centre is planned for the site. The north side of the street has changed greatly, the multiplicity of little family businesses having been swept away by the giant chain stores.

24. PRINCES STREET, looking west

Taken from the North British Hotel *c* 1905 this photograph epitomises the history and development of the city. The Castle set high on the ridge of the Old Town represents the beginnings of the city. The Waverley Market and Princes Street Gardens run along the valley of the Old Nor' Loch which had to be drained when the New Town was planned. The Mound, with its two fine galleries, the Royal Scottish Academy on Princes Street and the National Gallery behind, was originally a 'mud Brig' linking the two towns. Princes Street was one of the three main streets in James Craig's plan. The Scott Monument, is a reminder of the city's Golden Age of culture.

The modern view still has these reminders of Edinburgh's history and culture, but gives several clues to the 20th century city. Princes Street is a modern shopping centre with many large department stores; the traffic lights and lanes indicate the traffic congestion that is the scourge of the modern city. The Waverley Market in the foreground, has been demolished.

25. PRINCES STREET, east end

Using a wide-angled lens the photographer has given us a glimpse of the east end of Princes Street in the 1870s. His view from the Register House shows the equestrian statue of the Duke of Wellington, designed by Sir John Steele in 1852. The group of buildings on Princes Street includes the Bridge Hotel, Crawford the bakers, and the North British Railway Offices. The little arch at the extreme right is the entry to the Waverley Station. The horse tram is coming down the North Bridge where in the background we can see buildings being demolished, preparatory to the widening of the bridge in 1896. The large building to the left, on the corner of Princes Street and the North Bridge, is the General Post Office, erected on the site of the Theatre Royal, Shakespeare Square, in 1859.

Today the right-hand corner is completely dominated by the massive North British Station Hotel with its imposing clock tower. Built in 1902, it is one of the city's largest hotels.

26. NORTH BRIDGE, West Side

Probably taken in the 1880s before the North Bridge was rebuilt, this photograph shows the group of buildings on the west side of the bridge as it reaches its junction with Princes Street. The Register House, which faces the bridge, is visible in the background. Cranston and Elliot a well-known firm founded by Sir Robert Cranston (Lord Provost of Edinburgh from 1903-06), moved to Princes Street in 1895, probably due to the impending rebuilding of the North Bridge.

In 1875 the Waverley Station was being reconstructed, and as the piers of the North Bridge, which stood in the station, were found to be a hindrance to an efficient layout, the opportunity was taken to reconstruct the bridge and widen the road again (it was first widened in 1874 for the cable cars). In 1902 the North British Station Hotel was built on the site of Cranston and Elliot.

The modern photograph gives a clear view of the Register House which has been recently cleaned.

27. LEITH STREET

Leith Street was one of the city's liveliest streets leading from the North Bridge and the Old Town to the Port of Leith. It had many little shops in particular jewellers and shoe shops. An interesting feature was a terrace with additional shops on the right-hand side. In this view the side of the Georgian Register House can be seen with its small clock and behind it the huge clock tower of the North British Hotel.

Now Leith Street is virtually unrecognisable. All the shops not yet demolished will go shortly. In the place of the Terrace and St James Square which lay behind, a development has grown up which has caused endless controversy. The St James Shopping Centre dominates the east end of Princes Street. Its high tower blocks spoil the distant views of the city. It comprises shops, offices and the King James Hotel seen here. Many people feel that the looming mass of the St James Centre is an unfortunate companion for the delicate Adam architecture of the Register House.

28. GEORGE STREET

George Street, originally intended as the principal street in James Craig's plan for the New Town became, by chance, secondary to Princes Street. Here c1880 it was a street of family businesses, clubs and insurance companies. At the intersection with Castle Street stands one of the three George Street statues, that of Dr Chalmers, leader of the Disruption of the Church of Scotland.

Today the facade of the north side remains largely unchanged, although new shop fronts have been added. In recent years, the statues of Dr Chalmers, William Pitt and George IV have caused endless problems with traffic but so far have resisted all attempts to remove them. St George's Church, which was built in 1813, was one of the major New Town churches, and an integral part of the layout of Charlotte Square. In 1961 the Church was discovered to be infested with dry rot. In order to preserve the unity of Charlotte Square Edinburgh Corporation bought the building and have converted it into a public record office.

29. PIERSHILL BARRACKS

Built in 1793, Piershill Barracks stood in the country to the east of the city. In 1909 a survey was carried out which found that the accommodation was inadequate for 19 officers, 1 warrant officer, 35 married men, 383 men, 320 troop horses, 63 chargers, and that the proximity of the barracks to Craigentinny Meadows, an irrigated meadow, was unhealthy. The building was therefore condemned for cavalry purposes, and the Royal Scots Greys, one of whom can be seen at the main entrance were to leave the city.

The proposed removal of the Greys caused a public outcry, and led eventually to the construction of a new cavalry barracks at Redford. Piershill continued to be used by field regiments until 1934, when, with the departure of the 16th Brigade Royal Field Artillery, Edinburgh Corporation bought the site from the War Office. After clearing the eleven acre site, 340 working class houses were built, (using the stone from the barracks), around a square incorporating a bowling-green and a children's playground.

30. WEST PORT

The West Port which took its name from one of the old gates, or ports, in the city wall was one of the worst slums in Edinburgh in the 19th century. It was the haunt of criminals like Burke and Hare, the body-snatchers who lived in Tanners' Close. It was probably because of its reputation for vice and crime that Dr Chalmers, one of the pioneers of social reform and leader of the Disruption Movement of the Church of Scotland, carried out much of his work in this area. He founded a Territorial Church and School at the foot of the West Port and his Memorial Church can be seen on the south side of the street.

Argyle House, a huge block of government offices, covers the site where Burke and Hare carried out their grisly trade. The removal of other closes shows Portsburgh Square called after the ancient burgh of Portsburgh. Chalmers' Memorial Church has been demolished leaving a vacant site. Above the roofs of Portsburgh Square the Central Library is visible.

31. EARL GREY STREET

Probably taken at the same time as No. 32 when the photographer has swivelled his camera to the left, much to the interest of the three little boys standing at the edge of the pavement. This view from Tollcross is along Earl Grey Street showing the opposite end from that seen in No. 35.

It illustrates the great variety of little shops, particularly grocers, jewellers and ladies' outfitters that could be found there. Fleming's Stores, with household goods hanging outside, were a well-known landmark as was the Methodist Central Hall.

The buildings on the left can be readily recognised in the modern view, although the Clydesdale Bank occupies Campbell & Co's, Mantles and Costumes shop, and Fleming's Stores have been taken over by Shefco's dress shop. The right-hand side of Earl Grey Street, however (being part of the Tollcross clearance scheme), has recently disappeared completely. At the moment it is possible to see Lothian House, which stands on the site of Port Hopetoun, the old terminus of the Union Canal.

32. TOLLCROSS

Standing at Tollcross in 1914 the photographer has caught the essence of the period. A cable tram lurching out of Lauriston Place advocates the use of 'Beecham's Pills'. The Bill hoardings advise you to buy 'Nestle's', 'Fry's' and to attend 'The Empire' or the 'Palladium', twice nightly.

The place names belong to a much earlier era, 'High Riggs', the street to the left, being mentioned in a charter of 1387, and the 'Tollcross' in one of 1458. Both names are evocative, High Riggs denoting an elevated ridge of land, and Tollcross the cross at the toll. There is no trace of the toll or the cross today.

Through the clutter of street furniture we can see Goldbergs built in 1963 standing on the site of the old public house on the corner. Lauriston is now a clearance area and many of the tenements have already gone. Those remaining on the right are presently being demolished, but still standing on the left, is the local 'Buroo', the Employment Exchange.

33. FOUNTAINBRIDGE

The drawbridge at Fountainbridge will bring back a wave of nostalgia to many enthusiasts, for it is a reminder of the Union Canal. Built in 1822, the canal was a popular form of transport for goods and passengers, until the coming of the railways. Contemporary advertisements indicate that for 2/- cabin or 1/4d steerage you could travel all the way to Glasgow on the *Flora McIvor* which made 'swift passage at nine miles per hour'. The canal had two basins: Port Hopetoun was drained in 1922 and is now occupied by Lothian House; Port Hamilton was behind the building on the right.

Initially opened as a roller skating rink in 1909, it was converted to the Coliseum Cinema in 1911, and entered a period of great prosperity in 1920 when it was taken over by the Palais de Danse and Cinema Company. The bridge was removed in 1920 prior to the draining of Port Hopetoun and re-erected on another part of the Canal, at the foot of Leamington Road.

34. FOUNTAINBRIDGE

In early days Fountainbridge was an area of royal farms and orchards, commemorated in the names Castle Barns, King's Stables Road and Orchardfield. The name Fountainbridge first appeared on a tombstone in 1713 and the *Edinburgh Evening Courant* of 1774 refers to 'that fountain of excellent never-failing water from whence the street of Fountainbridge obtains its name'.

By 1912 the area had been built up completely. The canal basin behind the buildings on the left had brought various yards and offices with it. The names of the local shops, the 'River Plate Fresh Meat Company', 'Swift's Beef Company' and the 'Edinburgh Meat Market Company' are all reminders of the municipal slaughterhouse which stood on the right-hand side of the street. Built in 1851 it was removed to its present site at Gorgie in 1910.

Very little remains of old Fountainbridge.

35. EARL GREY STREET

Earl Grey Street in 1914 is typical of the Tollcross area of the city, with many little cut-price shops. Smart's tea-room would certainly provide that very Scottish institution 'high tea' — a cooked meal followed by scones, buns, and cakes. The street was given its high-flown name in an unusual way.

Called Wellington Street, after the Duke of Wellington, it had rather an abrupt change of name in 1834. Earl Grey, the prime minister who had done so much to bring about the Reform Act in 1832 was invited to the city in 1834. A great banquet was organised in his honour and during the evening some of the citizens who deplored Wellington's lack of support for reform, erased his name and substituted that of the Prime Minister.

It's difficult to recognise Earl Grey Street today. The tea-rooms, the tenements and the shops have all vanished. The tenements in Riego Street, which stood behind Earl Grey Street have a new view.

36. MORRISON STREET

Waldie's coalyard lay on the corner of Lothian Road and Morrison Street. A few steps through the archway led to Port Hopetoun, one of the basins of the Union Canal. The canal was built in 1822 to link Edinburgh and Glasgow by way of the Forth and Clyde Canal. Prior to 1822 Fountainbridge had been a rural area, but the canal brought industries with it and even though it was superseded by the railways in 1912, Fountainbridge remained mainly industrial.

An Act was passed in 1913 causing the North British Railway to give up that part of the Canal leading to the basin in Lothian Road. Consequently Port Hopetoun was drained in 1922, and in 1936 a large block of offices and shops was opened on the site.

In 1938 the Regal Cinema was opened exactly on the site of Waldie's yard. In 1969, to suit contemporary tastes, the large cinema was divided into three small cinemas and renamed the A.B.C. Film Centre.

37. CASTLE BARNS, MORRISON ST.

The area covered by the present-day Morrison Street was once covered by orchards, nursery gardens and farms, connected with the Castle. A map of 1798 shows Castle Barns as a small hamlet on the Falkirk Road. Maitland, in his 18th century *History of Edinburgh,* says that there was a building erected at Castle Barns to accommodate the royal retinue when the king was in residence at the Castle, but the name rather suggests that it was a grange, or farm attached to the fortress. Whatever its original purpose, even in 1912 it was clearly an interesting example of Scottish domestic architecture, with forestairs and pantiles.

Looking across Morrison Street from Semple Street today, we find that Castle Barns has vanished without trace, leaving in its place a sales area for second-hand cars.

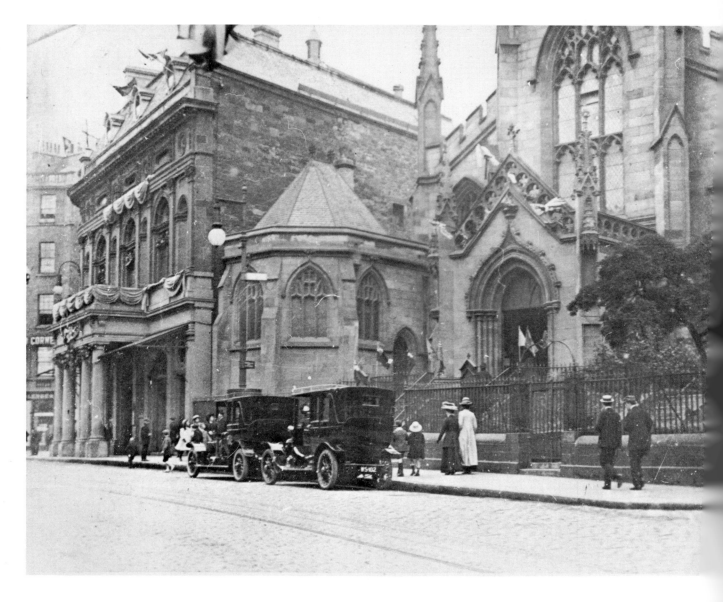

38. BROUGHTON STREET

Probably taken in 1911 during the visit of
George V and Queen Mary, this view shows
Broughton Street with flags flying. It looks
as if there might be a wedding in progress at
St Mary's Roman Catholic Cathedral.
Nearby the Theatre Royal is decorated for a
gala occasion.

St Mary's was designed in 1813 by
Gillespie Graham but has been altered
considerably since then. The Theatre Royal
was opened as a circus in 1790 and after
many changes of name, several fires and
restorations, it was finally burnt out in 1946.
The modern view shows one of the most
dramatic changes in the city. St Mary's
stands in isolation, dwarfed by the bulk of
the nearly completed St James Centre,
which covers the old St James Square and
one side of Leith Street. The strange object
in the foreground is a kinetic sculpture
which has been the subject of a lively
correspondence in the local press.

39. LEITH WALK

This fine view of Leith Walk in 1825 shows what a handsome street it must have been with a vista to Leith and the glassworks, the Firth of Forth and the shores of Fife. On the right, in Greenside Place, the Tabernacle, described in No. 40 can be seen next to the large Georgian buildings. At the junction with London Road the corner block with columns is part of the interesting layout for the area to the north of the Calton Hill. Beyond Leopold Place the line of trees explains why the street is called Elm Row.

Still a very wide street, Leith Walk has altered a great deal. The corner block at Leopold Place and Elm Row is still the same, although the elms have gone. The view to Leith is blocked by the high buildings; the spire of Pilrig Church is close to the old boundary between Edinburgh and Leith. The clock at the London Road roundabout should be familiar to inhabitants of Edinburgh, as it used to stand at the West End of Princes Street.

40. THE TABERNACLE, Greenside

The Tabernacle was a Baptist Meeting House which stood in Greenside Place in Leith Walk. It was used for meetings between 1801 and 1864, and such was the power of its preacher, James A. Haldane, that it had accommodation for 3,200 people (4,000 on special occasions). In 1864 the congregation moved to Duncan Street Baptist Church and the old hall became a furniture warehouse, occupied by J. Underwood, as shown in this view of 1914.

In 1929 another meeting place was built on the site of the Tabernacle, the Playhouse Cinema. It was one of the city's largest cinemas, with seating for over 3,000 people and for many years it enjoyed great popularity. Now however, the general decline in cinema-going has forced it to close recently. There has been considerable controversy over the fate of the building as some councillors have suggested that it could be used as an opera house, while others are in favour of demolition.

41. LEITH CENTRAL STATION

In the days of top hats and horse-transport the foot of Leith Walk was a popular meeting place, possibly because five main streets converged there. This view shows a horse tram swinging out of Constitution Street into Leith Walk; the top of the Kirkgate is visible on the left.

The Central Station has been empty and disused since 1952 but local councillors are making efforts to have an amenity centre opened in the building. Exiled Leith people returning to their old burgh would have difficulty in finding their bearings. The Kirkgate, once the hub of Leith life, is a slick shopping centre integrated with a huge housing development known as 'Banana Row'. The central block is not greatly changed. Smith and Bowman, the chemists, still remain in the same shop, and Woolworth have extended the property occupied by the Queen's Hotel. Dwarfing the old blocks, Kirkgate House with its giant television aerial is looking down on the New Leith.

42. 'THE FOOT OF THE WALK'

In the local idiom 'the foot of the Walk', is
the junction of Leith Walk, the Kirkgate,
Duke Street, Great Junction Street, and
Constitution Street. Leith was Edinburgh's
port from the 12th century and, in 1910, was
a bustling, thriving burgh. Many of its
industries were connected with the large
docks. The 'Leithers' had a real sense of
community, were very often inter-married,
and certainly did not consider themselves
citizens of Edinburgh.

In 1920 the Burgh of Leith was absorbed
into the City of Edinburgh and although the
buildings in this modern view have changed
very little, the spirit of the place is greatly
changed. Successive slum clearance schemes
have removed many of the inhabitants to the
suburbs, and as Leith Docks are being
overshadowed by Grangemouth further up
the Firth of Forth the whole area has lost its
busy atmosphere. Fortunately there are still
those who care about the past and future of
Leith, and organisations like Leith Civic
Trust are trying to preserve its heritage and
revive its community spirit.

43. LEITH, The Shore

The Water of Leith was Edinburgh's most important river, supporting many of the city's ancient industries (paper, snuff and flour mills) along its course. At the mouth of the river the town of Leith grew up, which was Edinburgh's port from the 12th century. Over the years intense rivalry developed between Edinburgh and Leith which heightened when Leith became a Burgh in 1833.

Before 1800, Leith had no docks and ships had to come into the harbour and tie-up alongside the quay which lined the river bank. As trade increased docks were eventually constructed between 1800 and 1817. The contrast between the two views illustrates exactly what has happened to Leith.

In the modern view the streets are deserted and the basin silent and empty. Even though the docks have been extended and modernised (the harbour was converted to a deep water port in the 1960s), Leith's importance has been usurped by Grangemouth further up the Forth.

44. OLD CATTLEMARKET

The old Cattlemarket, shown here in 1907, stood on the north side of Lauriston Place with the Castle in the background and the churches of St Cuthbert, St George and St John in the distance. The Cattlemarket was however a long way from a railway, causing great inconvenience to farmers, who had to drive their beasts through the streets to the slaughterhouse, at Fountainbridge. In 1910 it was finally closed when Edinburgh Corporation provided a new building at Gorgie. This brought the Cornmarket, the Slaughterhouse and the Cattlemarket under one roof.

In 1900 the Central Fire Station was built on part of the old Cattlemarket. In his opening address the Lord Provost, Mitchell-Thomson, made the point that Edinburgh had one of the first municipal brigades in the country. In 1907 Edinburgh College of Art, the building in the distance behind the trees, was opened on another part of the Cattlemarket. By 1910 all trace of the old market had gone.

45. GEORGE IV BRIDGE

George IV Bridge was built in 1836 bringing one of the roads from the south to the Old Town. By c1885 it had become a busy thoroughfare with horse trams, linking Princes Street to the Tollcross district and beyond. It was a popular site for public buildings, including the Old Midlothian County Buildings, which were built in 1818, and can be seen on the left.

Looking down George IV Bridge in 1974 it is obvious that there has been a considerable amount of change although the Augustine Bristo Church and the block beside it remain the same. The 1818 County Buildings were replaced in 1905, and in 1970 the County extended their premises to the opposite corner. The National Library of Scotland, opened in 1956, replaced the Sheriff Court, which was demolished in 1938. Directly opposite the National Library is the Central Library, built in 1890.

46. GEORGE IV BRIDGE

This view shows George IV Bridge in 1929. When it was built in 1836, several old closes on the south side of the Lawnmarket, including Liberton's Wynd, were demolished as a result. The bridge had eight arches, only two of which were open: one over Merchant Street and the other over the Cowgate.

The ornate building on the right is the Sheriff Court House, designed by David Bryce, and opened in 1868. Beyond the Court House is the entrance to the Advocates' Library, built on a lower level. On the corner of George IV Bridge and the Lawnmarket, the Midlothian County Buildings, opened in 1905, can be seen.

The Sheriff Court was demolished in 1938 and the National Library of Scotland, which was opened in 1956, was built on the site. The modern photograph gives a longer view showing the corner of the new Sheriff Court on the north side of the Lawnmarket and the dome of the Bank of Scotland. It illustrates how this road from the South formed a link, via Bank Street, to Princes Street.

47. BRISTO PLACE, c1930

Bristo Place seen here about 1930 stood on
the ancient lands of Bristo outside the
Flodden Wall. Although the area had a sad
neglected aspect by this time, many
interesting people were connected with it. In
the 18th century Mrs Maclehose, Robert
Burns's 'Clarinda', lived here in General's
Entry, and just a few yards from this scene
Robert Fergusson, Edinburgh's tragic
young poet, died in the local bedlam.
Nearby Windmill Street commemorates the
windmill built by the Town to pump water
for the use of the Society of Brewers. Due to
its position on one of the old roads leading
to the city, the inn in the centre of the
picture was used as stabling quarters for the
Carlisle Carriers. The building dated back
at least to 1741 but it was 1823 before the
landlord of the period, John Wilkinson,
named it 'The Woolpack'.

Even locals feel like visitors from another
planet when they drive round the
Bristo-One-Way-System today. Their only
point of reference is the McEwan Hall and
the line of bollards standing outside.

48. BRISTO PLACE, 1914

Taken in 1914 from a point near No. 47 in Bristo Place this view shows part of Teviot Row and the monument to William McEwan outside the McEwan Hall. The circular building in the foreground will be strange to most Edinburgh people because it was replaced by a curious half-timbered building know locally as 'Parker's Corner'. Beyond Bristo Street, the continuation of Bristo Place, the spire of Buccleuch Free Church can be seen. The building of the McEwan Hall in 1897 foreshadowed the future of the Bristo area.

In 1874 during one of its extension programmes the University expressed an urgent need for a hall but it was ten years later during the tercentenary celebrations before William McEwan, M.P., the owner of the brewing firm, offered to pay for a building. In the past few years Bristo Place, Bristo Street and Parker's Stores have been demolished by the University leaving a clear view to Buccleuch and Greyfriars Free Church; temporary car parks and Appleton Tower have taken their place.

49. GEORGE SQUARE

Built in 1766 by a speculative builder called James Brown, George Square, seen here in 1914, was the first large development outside the old city boundary and still encloses one of the largest open spaces of its kind in the city. Brown was very particular about the occupants of his houses and the early ones were 'perpetually restrained from dealing in, or the occupation of, any trade or merchandise'. The square had many distinguished occupants in its early days including Sir Walter Scott and Admiral Duncan, the hero of Camperdown. James Brown might be horrified to see the present tenants of his desirable properties. Large blocks of the Georgian buildings have been replaced by the William Robertson Building and behind it the Appleton Tower. In fact the square, which is being developed by the University, is occupied by students, sons and daughters of those dealing in trades and merchandise. The lovely central gardens have been retained and beyond them the Student Health Centre at Bristo can be seen.

50. NICOLSON STREET

Traffic duty was not very strenuous for the policeman in 1914, especially in the areas beyond the Old and New Towns. Built in the mid-18th century, Nicolson Street is a continuation of the South Bridge which links the North Bridge to the Old Town. At the junction with Crosscauseway and St Patrick Square, the working-class houses and shops are a feature of this district known locally as the 'South Side'. The area has been the subject of considerable controversy in recent years.

Although it is officially a clearance area the Nicolson Street traders and tenants have bitterly opposed the removal of their property which they feel is suitable for improvement, not demolition. The formation of amenity associations to defy the establishment is an interesting development in the modern city. The only features common to both views are the spires of Nicolson Street Church.

51. GRANGE LOAN

In 1854 Grange Loan, to the south of the
city, was clearly a country district. It was
part of the Grange, or farm of St Giles and
its mansion house, Grange House, dated
back to the 11th century. One of its most
famous visitors was Prince Charlie when he
was occupying the city in 1745. The house
was converted in the 19th century but
demolished in 1936 to make way for modern
bungalows. On the north side of the Loan,
the Penny Well, which is at least 200 years
old, was one of the main sources of water
supply for the people living on the south side
of the town. Hardly a country road today,
Grange Loan is one of the many residential
streets leading off Causewayside. Tenement
flats, grocers' shops and S.N.P. Committee
rooms have taken the place of the little
cottages, but just beyond the tenement
block one of the original villas is still
standing.

52. MERCHISTON CASTLE

This 18th century print shows Merchiston Tower when it stood in isolation near the Burgh Muir to the south of the Old Town. The lands of Merchiston can be traced back to the reign of Robert Bruce, but the Tower comes into historical record only in 1436 when it came into the possession of the Napier family. This family hold a distinguished place in Scottish history, including Lord Provosts and Ambassadors among their members. Undoubtedly the best known member was John Napier of Merchiston, the inventor of logarithms.

The estate passed through various hands until in 1833 Charles Chalmers, brother of Thomas Chalmers, the leader of the Disruption of the Church of Scotland founded Merchiston Castle School. The school remained there until 1930 and in 1934 the estate was acquired by the Town Council. For many years the Tower lay empty and derelict, but in 1964 after careful restoration it was integrated by the city Architect into a new building, aptly called Napier College.

Memory Lane

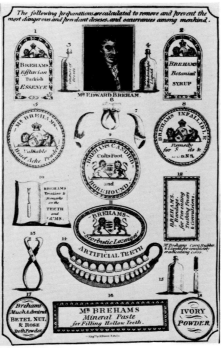

1. What excitement! Buffalo Bill and Annie Oakley performing at Gorgie in 1904. 140,000 people attended the exhibition, which later visited Falkirk, Dunfermline and Kirkcaldy.

2. Candid Camera, in 1908, visiting the Scottish National Exhibition at Saughton, Princes Street Gardens and Princes Street. What was an ironclad watch?

3. An artist's impression of the disaster at 'Heave-Awa' Land' in the High Street, when one of the high tenements collapsed in 1861 killing 35 people.

4. Edward Breham was certainly trying to provide a panacea for all ills. Headaches, toothache, burns, scurvy and corns all came within his scope, but his masterpiece must have been these artificial teeth.

5. The last stage coach to Leith outside Donaldson's, the tobacconist, at 73 Leith Walk in the 1870s.

6. One of the three-horse buses with iron-shod wheels which ran on the steep route between Stockbridge and Newington in the 1880s.

7. A cable car in Princes Street at the Waverley Steps on its way from Bernard Street in Leith to North Merchiston c1895.

8. Edinburgh's first taxi-cab, registered in 1907. This photo was taken in 1911.

9. A Scottish Motor Traction bus with gas-bag top used between Edinburgh and Penicuik during the First World War. It is seen on Waverley Bridge, 1916.

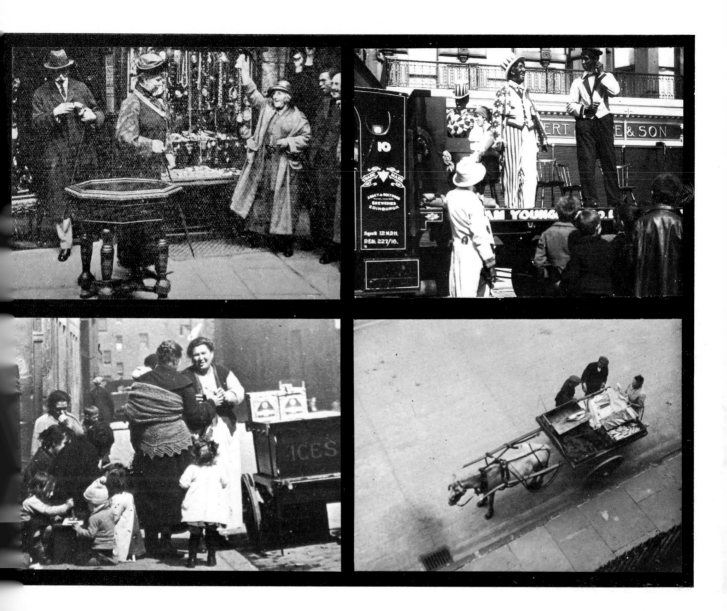

10. An enthusiastic cheer for Queen Mary as she leaves Henry's antique shop near John Knox's House in the High Street in 1914.

11. The Infirmary Pageant used to be an annual event. These minstrels have a rapt audience as they perform in Princes Street outside Maule's Shop, c1920.

12. A summer's day idyll in the Cowgate, 1924. Children at play and mother buying a delicious ice-cream cone. You can almost taste the raspberry flavouring that the Italian ice-cream lady is about to shake on to the cone.

13. Who'll buy my fresh fish? A street vendor in Lauriston Place, c1912.

14. A triumphal arch in Waterloo Place for the visit of Edward VII and Queen Alexandra in 1903.

15. A puffer steaming out of Waverley Station in 1934 with the Waverley and North Bridges in the background.

THE CITY CLEANED;
AND
COUNTRY IMPROVEN.

By following out this proposed
method, for paying only one
penny per week, for an 8 l.
rent, and so proportionally by
the possessors of each bounds,
consisting of 800 l. of yearly rent,
which is 50 houses, at 16 l. rent.

The city shall be flourishing,
her citizens abound
In number shall like to the grass
that grows upon the ground.
Psalm LXXII.

Act 12. Par. I. Sess. 2. Jam. VII.
an. 1686, intitled, cleaning the
streets.
That the Lords of Council and
Session do receive in such proposals
as their Lordships shall see to be effectu-
al, &c. &c. &c.

EDINBURGH,
MDCCLX.

N° 1

16. What a splendid idea! a scheme to charge householders a small amount in proportion to their annual rent to keep the city clean. Unfortunately it did not materialize and Edinburgh was notorious for 'Gardez-loo' (the practice, in the 18th century and earlier, of throwing slops out of the window into the street below, with a cry of 'Gardez-loo' — Garde de l'eau).

17. Perhaps the most famous dog in the world; Greyfriars' Bobby had a memorial fountain erected to him opposite Greyfriars' Churchyard where he had kept watch on his master's grave for 14 years, c1920.

18. A study in concentration as the little boy performs his ablutions at the 'jaw box' in Sandport Street, Leith in 1924.

19. Another study in water-supply in Sandport Street. Local housewives draw their water from the street well, 1924.